CUSTOMS · COSTUMES
AND CULTURES

COSTUMES

by
Kevin K. Casey

Rourke Publications, Inc.
Vero Beach, Florida 32964

ACKNOWLEDGEMENTS

I am grateful to Jerry Craven for many of the illustrations that appear throughout this book. I also thank Photophile of San Diego, California, and Picture Library Associates of Guadalupe, California, for the remaining photographs.

PHOTO CREDITS

© Photophile, L.L.T. Rhodes: pages 5, 23; © Picture Library Associates, Bess Grube Nelson: pages 6, 7; © Photophile, Jim Olive: page 8; © Jerry Craven: pages 8, 9, 14, 15, 20, 21, 29, 30; © Photophile, Jose Carrillo: pages 10, 17; © Photophile, Al Rodriguez: page 11; © Picture Library Associates, Sonia L. Garcia: page 12; © Photophile, Glasheen Graphics: page 13; © Photophile, J.L. Stangler: page 19; © Picture Library Associates, Dennis Fisher: page 22; © Picture Library Associates, Robert S. Mauck: page 25; © Photophile, Mark E. Gibson: page 26; © Photophile, Cheyenne Rouse: page 27

Library of Congress Cataloging-in-Publication Data

Casey, Kevin K., 1967-
    Costumes / by Kevin K. Casey.
        p.   cm. — (Customs, costumes, and culture)
    Includes index.
    Summary: Describes the clothing worn by different peoples
around the world for social, religious, and military purposes.
    ISBN 0-86625-596-6
    1. Costume—Juvenile literature. [1. Costume.] I. Title. II. Series.
GT518.C37   1996
391—dc20   96-21652
                                                     CIP
                                                     AC

Printed in the U.S.A.

TABLE OF CONTENTS

CHAPTER 1
From Animal Skins to Nylon

One of the first things people learned to do was make clothes. Thousands of years ago, just as today, people needed clothing to protect them from heat and cold. The earliest clothes were probably simple and made from animal skins. Later people learned better ways to use animal skins. Their clothing lasted longer and was more comfortable.

In addition to wearing clothing for protection, people began to wear clothing for other reasons. Some people wore clothing as decoration. Some groups of people became known for the type of clothing they wore, and they took pride in this. Making the group, or tribe's, clothing became an important job.

Some people made clothing from plants. They made leaves and grasses into many different kinds of clothes. Though not as strong or warm as animal skins, clothing made from leaves or grass was easy to make. When the clothes wore out, there was plenty of material to make more.

Once people learned to weave, wool from sheep became a popular material for clothing. After people from Europe moved to North and South America, cotton became an important source of clothing material. Cotton is light but strong. Both cotton and wool are still popular today.

The newest materials for clothing are synthetic—made by people—like nylon. Synthetic materials do not come from plants or animals. Everything from winter coats to women's stockings can be made from synthetic materials.

As with other people all over the world, American cowboys still wear clothing similar to that of their ancestors.

CHAPTER 2
On Top of the World

There is a group of people who live on top of the world in an area called Lapland. In northern Norway, Sweden, Finland, and in the Kola peninsula of Russia, Lapps—or Laplanders—live the way they have for thousands of years.

In Norway, the western part of Lapland, there are deep rocky inlets from the sea called **fjords** (fee YORDZ). In the eastern parts of Lapland there are rolling hills and thousands of lakes. The land might be different, but one thing is true for all of Lapland: it is always cold.

These Laplanders in northern Norway wear colorful, warm clothing.

Many Lapps raise reindeer. This Laplander woman takes care of a newborn reindeer.

Many Laplanders are **nomads** (NOH madz). They move from place to place, following herds of reindeer. The reindeer provide much of the material needed for the Laplanders' warm and colorful clothing.

All Laplander clothing protects the Laplanders from the cool Arctic summers and the bitter cold Arctic winters. Much of Laplander clothing comes from reindeer. Perhaps the most interesting items of Laplander clothing are their shoes. Laplander shoes are made from reindeer skins. They do not have laces, and Laplanders do not wear socks. Instead of socks, they put grass inside their shoes. Laplanders prefer grass to cloth socks because the grass stays warm, even when it gets wet.

CHAPTER 3
Nomads of the Desert

In Saudi Arabia there are tribes of people called **bedouins** (BEH duh wunz). The bedouins are nomads, and they live their entire lives wandering through the Arabian Desert. The Arabian Desert is one of the hottest and driest places in the world. Only the bedouins can survive there. The bedouins know where to find water in the desert. A place in the desert with water is called an *oasis.*

Bedouins wear clothes that keep them cool during the hot days of summer. Bedouin men wear loose fitting robes. They cover their heads with cloth held in place by a band of wool. The cloth helps shield the men from the hot desert sun.

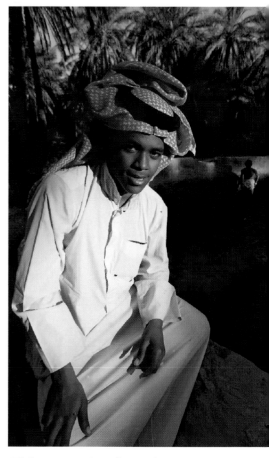

This young Saudi Arabian relaxes at a desert oasis.

These Islamic women wear traditional clothing and veils to hide their faces.

These Muslims kneel before an **imam,** *an Islamic or religious leader, in New Delhi, India. The imam gives blessings in exchange for donations for the poor.*

The bedouin women also wear long robes. In addition to cloth covering their heads, bedouin women wear black veils that hide all of the face except the eyes and forehead.

Part of the reason bedouin women dress the way they do is because of their religion, which is called **Islam** (is LAHM). Other Islamic women all over the world dress like the bedouin women. Arab women throughout the Middle East and Africa wear robes and veils, and so do Islamic women in India and Southeast Asia.

These Islamic college students in Malaysia wear traditional clothing. Unlike other Muslims, these women do not wear veils. In the background is The Great Blue Mosque near the city of Kuala Lumpur.

CHAPTER 4
The Chinese Princess in Mexico

The traditional costumes for the jarape tapaio *are the* charro *for the men and the* china poblana *for the women.*

In Mexico, traditional costumes help the Mexican people remember their past. Most Mexican costumes date back to the days of the Spanish colonists, and some costumes come from the time before the first Europeans arrived in Mexico.

This Mexican woman makes clothing the traditional way on a strap loom.

The traditional costume is important to Mexico's national dance, the *jarape tapaio* (ha RA pe TA pay yoh). The jarape tapaio is a lively and beautiful dance. Women wear the *china poblana* (KIN a po BLA na), and men wear the *charro* (CHA ro), or Mexican cowboy costume. The charro is made of tight fitting pants with **embroidery** (im BROY duh ree) and metal buttons. The male dancers also wear short jackets, neckerchiefs, and a big black sombrero.

The women's costume, or china poblana, has a long and interesting history from the Mexican town of Puebla. Legend states that many years ago a Chinese princess was rescued from pirates by a merchant ship on its way to Mexico. Though the princess was happy to escape from the pirates, she missed her home country while she was stranded in Mexico. To cure her homesickness, she decorated her blouses with embroidery that pictured scenes from China. From that time on, the Chinese princess was called "china poblana," or "Chinese girl from Puebla." The beautiful blouses she wore became popular with Mexican women. Soon after it became a tradition to decorate blouses with colorful embroidery.

CHAPTER 5
The Tigre Dance

Many cultures use costumes in celebrations. Throughout Mexico, every town and village has several fiestas every year. In most fiestas there are celebrations that include costumes. Sometimes these celebrations are dances. Other times they are plays that tell a story.

There are several reasons for these celebrations. The most common are for telling a community's history, religious festivals, and insuring good crops.

One of the most amazing celebrations is the *tigre* dance. The tigre dance tells a story with many characters. The dancers in the tigre dance wear costumes with masks that look like the heads of the characters they play. The two most important characters are the dog and the cat.

This Mexican-American girl in her beautiful dress prepares for a fiesta.

Some dancers in central Mexico wear elaborate costumes with long feathers.

The cat, or tigre, is not a small cat, like a house cat, but a ferocious beast, like a mountain lion or jaguar. The dog stands for animals that are friendly to humans, like horses, cows, and dogs. The tigre stands for dangers to humans, like a wild cat that might eat people tending their crops.

In the tigre dance, the dog is the hero. The dog leads the other characters to the fierce tigre. There they kill the tigre and make the land safe for everyone.

CHAPTER 6
Clothing in India and Nepal

Indians in traditional clothing shop for food at a market in Jaipur, India.

Some clothes show how important a person is. For instance, the color of a shawl and the way it is worn might reveal a person's social status, or wealth. In Nepal cotton is common among the lower classes, while the wealthier classes prefer silk.

The *sari* is perhaps the best-known costume for women. The sari has three parts. The first part covers the woman's upper body, but leaves her stomach bare. The second part is a long skirt. The third, or sari piece, is a long section of cloth 18 to 30 feet long. The sari wraps around the waist and drapes over one shoulder.

These men in Katmandu, Nepal, sell fruit at a street market.

Buddhist monks are another common sight in India and Nepal. Buddhist monks do not care about money or other material possessions. They spend much of their time in silent meditation. Meditation is the practice of deep breathing and concentration on only one thing. Buddhist monks wear simple clothes, and they are easy to identify in their bright orange robes.

The most typical clothes for men in Nepal and the northern regions of India are long, robelike cotton or wool garments that gather at the waist with a sash. These clothes are warm, and that is important because this part of the world is in the Himalayan Mountains, the highest mountains in the world.

Young women in Katmandu, Nepal, wear eye makeup to keep away evil spirits.

CHAPTER 7
Dragon Robes

The color of traditional clothing was important in China. The color of clothing could tell how influential or important a person was. Color could also have other meanings. In traditional Chinese clothing, red and gold stood for happiness, wealth, and good luck. Blue and green were colors women often wore. Yellow was another important color. Only the emperor could wear yellow clothes.

Probably the most famous of all traditional Chinese costumes were the "dragon robes." Dragon robes were beautiful silk robes that went all the way to the floor. The emperor's dragon robe was the most beautiful. The emperor's robe had embroidery of the sea, mountains, and sky. This meant that the emperor was important to both heaven and Earth.

China is large country. China also has the most people of any country in the world. Even though it is such a big country with so many people, China's traditional costumes are often the same throughout the land. Clothing in the warm southern regions is made from lightweight material like silk. In the cold northern regions, clothes are made from warmer material. The costumes in one place might look the same as the costumes in another Chinese town 1,000 miles away, even if they are made with different materials.

These young Chinese-American women wear traditional costumes while performing a dance in a public park.

CHAPTER 8
The Kimono

The kimono is the best-known Japanese costume. The kimono is a robe with large sleeves, which is tied or worn open. Both Japanese women and men wear kimonos. Today, men usually wear kimonos only at home or while relaxing, but many Japanese women wear kimonos as everyday clothing. The most beautiful kind of women's kimono is the wedding kimono.

Most kimonos are made of silk or cotton, but some are lined or quilted for colder weather. The beautiful kimonos that Japanese women wear have two kimonos: an inner and an outer kimono. The outer kimono is ankle length, and it is held in place by a sash called an *obi*. An obi is 1 foot wide and 15 feet long. The obi wraps around the woman's body several times.

When wearing kimonos, most Japanese wear *tabi*. Tabi are white socks that fit between the toes. Many Japanese also wear wooden sandals. These sandals are called *geta* or *zori* sandals. The Japanese wear the geta or zori sandals outdoors, but not in the house.

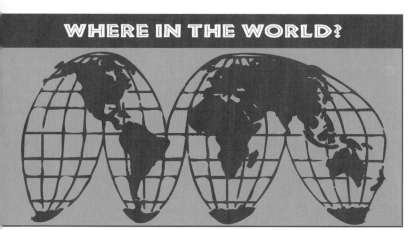

WHERE IN THE WORLD?

Many women in Japan still wear the kimono as everyday clothing.

CHAPTER 9
Southeast Asian Costumes

Buddhist monks in Chiang Mai, Thailand, meditate in their traditional orange robes.

Southeast Asia is a large area of the world with many different climates and cultures. In the west it begins at Burma's border with India. It goes east through southern China, and through all of the Asian countries south of China.

The land and climate of Southeast Asia changes from place to place. There are high mountains and deep valleys. There are jungles and tropical coastal areas. Each different area has a different climate. The people of Southeast Asia wear clothes that fit their environment.

This woman is part of a group of Malaysian people called the "Orang Osli," or "original people." The Orang Osli lived in Malaysia before other Asian people came south. This woman works on a rubber plantation.

The many kinds of clothes and costumes in Southeast Asia also change because of the many religions in the area. In addition to local religions, Buddhism, Islam, and Confucianism have many followers. Just as in India, Buddhist monks in Southeast Asia wear orange robes. Islamic women in Southeast Asia wear long robes and a cloth that covers their heads, just like the Islamic women in the Middle East.

In much of Southeast Asia, both men and women wear a wrap-around skirt called a *sarong*. The sarong got its start in southern China, but today it is popular in many other countries, including Malaysia. In Malaysia, many people combine the sarong with clothing from other areas of the world, such as Chinese jackets or Muslim turbans.

This woman on the Indonesian island of Sumatra is taking a chicken to market. She will trade the chicken for goods and carry them home in the basket on her head.

CHAPTER 10
Clothes Made from Leaves

For hundreds of years, Polynesians made much of the cloth they used for clothing from plants. Since they lived on warm tropical islands, Polynesian men wore only a loincloth, a small garment that covered only the waist and hip area. Polynesian women wore short skirts.

When the first Polynesians traveled to New Zealand, they could not find the plants they had used on other islands. This posed an even greater problem since the islands of New Zealand were not as warm as the islands the Polynesians had come from. The newcomers needed clothing to protect them from the cold.

Fijian men perform a traditional dance.

This Maori woman dances while wearing a traditional costume. The Maori live on the islands of New Zealand.

The Maori are descendants of the Polynesians who first traveled to New Zealand. They discovered a plant with leaves that they could make into soft, but strong, clothes. After they scraped leaf fibers with sea shells, they washed them and beat them with rocks. Then Maori women wove them into clothing. The Maori women also used the same type of leaf to make fishing nets and ropes.

The Maori chiefs of New Zealand wore cloaks made from the skin of dogs. The Maori chiefs also put feathers from beautiful birds on these cloaks.

CHAPTER 11
The Plain People

In parts of Pennsylvania, Ohio, Indiana, Wisconsin, and Canada, a group of people called the Amish still live the way their ancestors did over 300 years ago. The Amish are sometimes called the "Plain People," and they lead simple lives.

The clothing of the Amish is not the only thing "simple" in their lives. The Amish do not drive cars. Instead, they travel in buggies pulled by horses. Amish families live in simple wooden homes without many of the things most American families take for granted. There are no mirrors, pictures, radios, televisions, or phones in Amish homes.

The traditional clothing of the Amish is also simple. Men wear black coats without collars. The coats fasten with hooks, not buttons. Amish men also wear black wide-brimmed hats, black trousers and black boots. Amish men do not wear mustaches. However, after they are married, all Amish men wear beards. The Amish women's clothing is like the Amish men's. Women wear long black coats over long dresses with high collars. They also wear black bonnets over white prayer caps.

Amish children lead a very different life than most other children in the U.S. They go to school in one-room schoolhouses, with all the grades together. Amish teachers concentrate on teaching the basics—reading, writing, and arithmetic. Amish children learn to speak both English and German. They only go to school through the eighth grade. Most finish school by age 14.

An Amish boy and his father dress in simple traditional clothing. The Amish do not drive cars. Instead they travel in black buggies like the ones pictured in the background.

THE FIRST AMISH

The Amish community began way back in 1693. A man named Jacob Amman felt his church, the Mennonites, were not following their beliefs closely enough. He believed that God wanted people to do God's work. Worldly things—such as today's televisions and cars—could only get in the way. He and his followers separated from the Mennonites and formed their own religious group—the Amish.

CHAPTER 12
Remembering the Past

Making and wearing traditional costumes is one way that Native Americans preserve their heritage. The Pueblo Indians of New Mexico still wear clothes like those they have worn for many centuries.

Before the Spanish moved into what is now New Mexico, many Pueblo Indians made their clothes from cotton. In the areas near the Rio Grande River, some Pueblo Indians raised cotton.

Some Native Americans wear traditional headdresses at festivals that celebrate Native American heritage.

Traditional dances are an important part of preserving Native American heritage.

It was hard to make clothing from cotton plants, and it took a long time. During the winter, families took the seeds out of the cotton. Then the men made the cotton into thread and wove the thread into clothing for the entire family. The women made some clothing, like moccasins, as well as mats and baskets.

After the Spanish came to New Mexico, the Pueblo Indians learned to make clothes from wool. Today, many women still wear a robe garment called a *manta*, made from wool.

Many Hopi Indians still wear traditional costumes. The men still make most of the clothing worn by the tribe. The men even sew the beautiful embroidery into the clothes. One famous Hopi specialty is the rain sash. Rain sashes are white belts with long tassels. The long waving tassels stand for rain.

CHAPTER 13
Uniforms

An important type of costume is the uniform. The most common reason people wear uniforms is for their occupation, or job. Police wear blue uniforms so everyone can recognize, trust, and respect them. Medical doctors wear white coats, and some restaurant chefs still wear large white hats.

Another reason people wear a uniform is for protection. Fire fighters wear red hats and yellow coats for protection from fire. Construction workers wear hard hats, sturdy boots, and gloves to protect them from heavy construction equipment.

Still another reason people wear uniforms is for the sake of tradition. Some occupations have used the same uniform for a long time. Gurkha soldiers from Nepal that serve in the Indian or British armies have worn the same style uniform for centuries. Gurkha soldiers take pride in their reputation as fierce warriors. The uniform they wear is a part of that tradition.

Other soldiers around the world take pride in their uniforms, too. The United States Marines take great care in wearing their dress uniform. A Marine's dress uniform is always pressed, and every button and metal buckle is always polished and shining.

In their colorful traditional uniforms, these Gurkha soldiers guarding a palace in India pose with American tourists.

CHAPTER 14
Costumes Then and Now

Today, just like thousands of years ago, people need clothing for protection from heat and cold. Modern people also wear clothing as decoration. Some people wear special clothes to celebrate their heritage, and other people wear clothes to show their status in society. Many people choose clothing for comfort.

As time passes, people design and wear new forms of clothes, but the old forms and styles also stay popular. The materials used to make clothes keep getting better. Mountain climbers and astronauts wear clothes and uniforms made from the latest synthetic materials. Other people, like the Amish or some Native Americans, prefer to dress like their ancestors.

This woman in Nepal wears a warm coat over the traditional sari.

GLOSSARY

bedouins (BEH duh wunz) – nomadic Arabs of the desert.

charro (CHA ro) – the traditional Mexican cowboy costume.

china poblana (KIN a po BLA na) – the traditional costume for women worn for the national dance of Mexico.

embroidery (im BROY duh ree) – the art of sewing designs into cloth.

fjord (fee YORD) – a long and narrow inlet from the sea bordered by high rocky cliffs.

Islam (is LAHM) – the religion of Muslims; the religion that began in the late 500s A.D. in Arabia.

jarape tapaio (ha RA pe TA pay yoh) – the national dance of Mexico.

nomad (NOH mad) – a person or tribe with no permanent home who wanders from place to place.

INDEX